They All Lived in Redding

Caption from the original 18th century etching: House in Redding, (formerly Gen. Putnam's Quarters.)

They All Lived in Redding

The People and Places of This Extraordinary Town

For the past three centuries Redding has been a magnet for many notable people who have discovered Redding's magical qualities. This book recognizes one hundred of them.

Dennis Paget

Copyright © 2008 by Dennis Paget.

Book design: John A. DeCesare

Front cover: photograph of Redding Center by Redding photographer, Henry Polio

Front cover design by Martine Leroux

Photograph of Mark Twain courtesy of Reddingite Heather Morgan. Detail from a painting by Redding artist, Susan Durkee

Library of Congress Control Number: 2007909829
ISBN: Hardcover   978-1-4363-0979-0
             Softcover   978-1-4363-0978-3

All rights reserved. No part of this book may be reproduced or transmitted in any form or by any means, electronic or mechanical, including photocopying, recording, or by any information storage and retrieval system, without permission in writing from the copyright owner.

This book was printed in the United States of America.

To order additional copies of this book, contact:
Xlibris Corporation
1-888-795-4274
www.Xlibris.com
Orders@Xlibris.com
44802

This book is dedicated to my incomparable wife and life partner, Nancy Pelz-Paget, for her constant devotion, patience, and support through our years together—and especially during the writing of this book.

"How beautiful it all is! I did not think it could be as beautiful as this."

The words of Mark Twain in 1908, upon surveying the countryside from his new home in Redding, as quoted in "Mark Twain, a Biography" by Albert Bigelow Paine.

Why I love Redding

I have lived in Redding for more than twenty years and every day I spend here, I think to myself how fortunate I am to have discovered this special part of the world. This book is also dedicated to all those whose efforts have kept Redding the naturally beautiful town it is.

With its rolling wooded acres and historic white colonials and churches, Redding is a picture of the classic, unspoiled New England town.

For years Connecticut Magazine has designated Redding as the Number One Small Town in Connecticut.

Redding has just about everything one could want in a place to live.

- If you want natural beauty and tranquility, we have it, like few other places you can find nearer than Vermont.
- If you want great schools for your children you've come to the right place.
- If you're looking for active sports we have golf, tennis, swimming, hiking, cross-country skiing and many playing fields for other sports.
- If you're looking for an evening of fun and music the Redding Roadhouse and The Georgetown Saloon could keep you up late at night.
- Our many houses of worship will satisfy most religious persuasions.
- It's all here! Read further to discover the remarkable diversity offered by this town of fewer than 9,000 people.

The Town of Redding, first settled around 1711, was officially incorporated in 1767. It was originally called "Reading," after one of its early settlers, John Read, a landowner and lawyer. In 1714, Mr. Read obtained 500 acres of land from sachem Chickens Warrups, a Sagamore leader of displaced Paugussett and Pawtootuck Indians. In 1749, Chickens exchanged his tribe's remaining 200 acres of Redding land for 100 acres in Kent which is where they then moved. Warrups's grandson Tom remained in the area and later served as a scout under General Israel Putnam in the Revolutionary War.

THEY ALL LIVED IN REDDING

Joel Barlow, poet, patriot, political writer, and statesman, was born in Redding in 1754. He studied law and later became a political writer in the U.S. and England. In 1787, he wrote his epic poem, "The Vision of Columbus," which made him famous. In 1811, Barlow served as Minister to France and was invited by Napoleon, then absent on his Russian campaign, to meet him in Wilna, Poland, where a treaty, whose terms had been agreed upon, would be signed. Barlow set out, but on reaching Wilna, found Napoleon in retreat. Becoming involved in the retreat, Barlow was overcome by cold and privation, and died in Yarmisica, Poland in 1812. Barlow counted Thomas Jefferson, James Madison, and Robert Fulton among his friends. Joel Barlow High School in Redding is named in his honor.

Mark Twain (Samuel Clemens) at the age of 71 purchased land, sight unseen, in Redding because his biographer, Albert Bigelow Paine, lived here. Twain contracted an architect to design a house for him and his family. He did not want to see it, he said, until "the cat is purring on the hearth." When his house was completed, arriving by train, he was greeted by the flower-bedecked vehicles of local residents and entertained that night with fireworks.

Twain approved of the two-story Italian-style villa, with the red-walled billiard room, that he soon dubbed "Stormfield" after the story "Captain Stormfield's Visit to Heaven" that helped to fund the house. He spent the last two years of his life at Stormfield reading, writing, and playing billiards until his death in 1910.

Today, one can walk on trails through much of what was Twain's property. (The town bought 160 acres of the 248 original acres.) The Stormfield house that was located at the end of what is now Mark Twain Lane, burned down in 1923 and today much of the original property is privately owned. The town's Mark Twain Library was founded by the author, who also donated some books from his own personal collection.

THEY ALL LIVED IN REDDING

Edward Steichen is perhaps best remembered for his fashion, celebrity and documentary photography. After World War II, Steichen became Director of Photography at the Museum of Modern Art. This included in 1955 the organization of what became one of the most popular exhibitions in the history of photography, "The Family of Man." In 1964 the Edward Steichen Photography Center was established in the museum. Less well known is that he originally purchased land in Redding in 1929 and spent weekends at his home on Topstone Road. Many years later in Redding he cultivated delphiniums and began his painting career. He exhibited his artwork at the Museum of Modern Art until his death in West Redding in 1973. Steichen constructed Topstone Pond, which now serves as the town beach and swimming area. The house and most of his property are now privately owned.

Barlow, Twain, and Steichen are just three of the many creative people who have drawn inspiration from living in Redding. The Town also attracts business executives commuting to New York or nearby towns, professionals working at home, families seeking high-quality education for their children, and others looking for a bucolic retreat.

Whether through word-of-mouth, a fall foliage tour around the reservoir, a hike through one of its many public trails, or a methodical search for a country home, people are discovering this quiet green haven in the north of Fairfield County, and they often stay. Redding is one of the least dense towns in Connecticut, with a population of around 8,700, covering its 32.2 square miles. But Redding doesn't suffer isolation: opportunities abound in Redding and neighboring towns for seasonal, athletic, cultural and other community activities.

THEY ALL LIVED IN REDDING

FAMOUS AND ENDURING REDDINGITES

Charles Ives—1912 to 1954, Widely regarded as one of the first American classical composers of international significance. The Charles Ives Music Center in Danbury holds concerts every summer (lived on Umpawaug Hill)

Jascha Heifetz—1940's to 1950's, Considered one of the greatest violinists who ever lived. Throughout his life he was known for his flawless technical style. He recorded 80 albums (lived on Sanfordtown Rd)

Leonard Bernstein—1950's to 1964, Composer, orchestra conductor, pianist. He is renowned for both his conducting of the New York Philharmonic, and his Broadway theatrical musicals, including "West Side Story," "Candide" and "On The Town" (lived on Fox Run Rd)

Anna Hyatt Huntington—1930's to 1973, Sculptor, whose works grace the Mark Twain Library, Huntington Park, Putnam Park and two local schools. She and her husband donated the land for Huntington Park, which lies in Redding, Bethel, and Newtown (lived on Sunset Hill Rd)

Archer Huntington—1930's to 1955, Founded the Hispanic Society of America, art collector, museum founder, philanthropist. He and Anna donated the land for Huntington Park (lived on Sunset Hill Rd)

John Read—Early 1700's-1722, Lawyer who settled in the Redding area. He was a minister in Waterbury, Hartford and Stratford. Became the Queen's Attorney in 1708, was on Connecticut's Committee to revise the laws in May 1709. He moved to Massachusetts in 1722 and became the Massachusetts Attorney General. Born in 1679/1680 and died in 1749 (lived on Putnam Park Rd)

**REDDING CENTER WITH CONGREGATIONAL CHURCH
AND HISTORIC COLONIALS**

Redding has four main regions:

Redding Center:

Next to Town Hall is Redding Green and across the road is the Redding Center Post Office and the Town Hall Annex. Further down the road is the Old Town House, and the Congregational Church is near the flagpole where town ceremonies are held. Down Lonetown Road are the Elementary School, the Redding Community Center (sits behind the school), the Redding Historical Society, and the Redding Country Club.

West Redding:

Marked by the West Redding Post Office and a small group of shops and the train station, where Mark Twain first arrived in Redding to see his newly-built home and where commuters today grab a quick muffin and coffee before boarding the train for points south.

Georgetown:

A designated part of Redding, Ridgefield, Wilton, and Weston, and provides quick access to stores, gas stations, restaurants, and other essential businesses. It is home to the former Gilbert & Bennett wire mill. Georgetown is being developed into a pedestrian-friendly village that will include, single family homes, townhouses, lofts, affordable senior housing, retail and commercial businesses, a community theater, a health club and a new railroad station.

Redding Ridge:

Route 58 serves as the main thoroughfare coming from Fairfield to the south, Easton to the east, and Bethel to the north, a stretch of which has been designated for Federal status as one of America's scenic routes. Joel Barlow High School, which serves Redding and Easton students, is along Route 58.

THEY ALL LIVED IN REDDING

DISTINGUISHED AND WELL-KNOWN REDDINGITES

David Lilienthal—1950's, Scientist, Chairman of the Atomic Energy Commission, Director of Tennessee Valley Authority (lived on Stepney Rd)

Stuart Chase—1930's to 1980's, Economist, engineer, philosopher, land-use activist. author, helped found Consumer's Union. His book "A New Deal" was the term adopted by President Franklin D. Roosevelt (lived on Redding Rd)

Albert Bigelow Paine—1900's to 1930's, Author, editor, official biographer and friend of Mark Twain (lived on Diamond Hill Rd)

Nobel Hoggeson—1910's to 1930's, Architect. He rebuilt the Poverty Hollow area of Redding Ridge and was responsible for the stone bridge near the base of Church Hill Rd. that is now on the National Register. He edited Hoggeson's Journal, an architectural journal that used examples from the restorations he did in Poverty Hollow.

Rosamond Bernier—1970's to 2002, World-renowned art lecturer, founded the influential art magazine L'Oeil in Paris in 1955. Author of "Matisse, Picasso, Miro, as I Knew Them," awarded a Chevalier de la Légion d'Honneur, and the highest Spanish honor, the Order of Isabel la Católica (lived on Poverty Hollow Rd)

John Russell—1970's to 2002, Former chief art critic of the New York Times, author, awarded a Chevalier de la Légion d'Honneur (lived on Poverty Hollow Rd)

A WATERFALL NEAR MARK TWAIN LANE

COMMUNITY SERVICES & ORGANIZATIONS

**STEICHEN POND AT TOPSTONE PARK
FOR SWIMMING AND CANOEING**

The Park and Recreation Department offers over 60 programs each year geared to preschoolers, school-age children, teens, and adults. Four times a year the Department mails a brochure to every resident listing current offerings that include:
Aerobic and tennis lessons, summer concerts on Redding Green, swimming at Topstone Park, town tennis courts, skiing, canoe trips, men's softball league, annual plant sale on Redding Green, violin lessons, lifeguard instruction, yoga classes, summer day camp, creative writing classes, gymnastics, Broadway outings, open gym, tennis tournament, quilting, bridge.

ANNUAL GARDEN CLUB PLANT SALE

SENIOR CITIZEN SERVICES
Heritage Community Center
Education courses
Special guest lectures
Weekly luncheons
Healthcare screenings
Friends Visitor Program
Meals-on-Wheels programs
Town-funded van service

THEY ALL LIVED IN REDDING

DISTINGUISHED AND WELL-KNOWN REDDINGITES

Igor Kipnis, 1980's to 2002, World-renowned harpsichordist, forte pianist, director, music teacher (lived on Drummer Lane)

Joseph Wood Krutch. 1940's, literary naturalist, author, drama critic (lived on Limekiln Rd)

Alfred Winslow Jones—1970's to 1989, Created the first financial hedge fund, sociologist, and journalist (lived on Poverty Hollow Rd)

Maurice Pate—1940's to 1965, First Executive Director of UNICEF. Under Pate's leadership, UNICEF grew to be the UN's most famous and respected agency, providing food and medical aid for a hundred million children worldwide (lived on Putnam Park Rd)

Dan Beard—1908 to 1930's, Boy Scouts of America's first commissioner and the illustrator for Mark Twain's "A Connecticut Yankee in King Arthur's Court" (lived on Great Pasture Rd)

Elmo Roper—1950's to 1971, Pioneer in the fields of market research and public opinion polling, the first to develop the scientific poll for political forecasting (lived on Chestnut Hill Rd)

Walter White—1940's to 1950's, one of the most important civil rights leaders of the first half of the twentieth century. He was Executive Secretary of the NAACP (lived on Seventy Acres Rd)

Elizabeth Janeway—1980's, Writer, wrote seven novels and her novel, "Daisy Kenyon" became a major motion picture, served as President of the Authors Guild, Janeway was the original inspiration for the character Kathryn Janeway of "Star Trek: Voyager," the first female lead in the Star Trek series (lived on Poverty Hollow Rd)

Eliot Janeway—1980's, Political economist. Economic adviser to Presidents Franklin D. Roosevelt and Lyndon B. Johnson, syndicated columnist, published two important economic newsletters, wrote many books (lived on Poverty Hollow Rd)

CHRIST CHURCH WITH OLD GRAVESTONES

RELIGIOUS SERVICES

The tall white spires of many of Redding's churches serve as important landmarks in Redding's history, architecture, and geography.

Baptist—Calvary Independent Baptist
Bible—Georgetown Bible Church
Buddhist Meditation Center and DNKL Tibetan Buddhist Center for Universal Peace
Catholic—Sacred Heart and St. Patrick
Benedictine Grange
Congregational—UCC, First Church of Christ, Congregational
Eckankar Center of Fairfield County
Episcopal—Christ Church
Jewish—B'nai Chaim
Lutheran—Bethlehem (ELCA)
Methodist—Georgetown and Long Ridge
Unitarian Universalist Congregationalist (Danbury)

REDDING COUNTRY CLUB AND GOLF COURSE

OTHER ACTIVITIES AND ORGANIZATIONS

Recreation Department

Redding Land Trust—
   Founded in 1965 in order to preserve Redding's natural heritage of open space. Today the RLT holds some 1,600 acres of meadows and woodlands, saved forever from the bulldozer

New Pond Farm—
   a non-profit environmental education center that provides opportunities to learn about and appreciate natural science, Native-American heritage, farming traditions, astronomy and the arts. Founded by Carmen Mathews, an actress who lived on this property for many years

Redding Country Club and golf course

Redding Garden Club

Boys and Girls Club

Boy Scouts

Girl Scouts

Redding Neighbors & Newcomers Club

Redding League of Women Voters

The Redding Preservation Society—
   Dedicated to the preservation of antique Redding structures

The Redding Historical Society—
   Maintains a one-room brick schoolhouse, Umpawaug Schoolhouse, listed in the National Register of Historic Places and Lonetown Farmhouse/Museum

The Redding Pilot—
   The town's weekly newspaper.

MARK TWAIN LIBRARY

Mark Twain Library—Mark Twain spearheaded the establishment of a town library soon after he arrived in June 1908. It was opened quite humbly in a small unused chapel in September 1908 with books donated by Twain and with Twain as President. He held a fund-raising concert and posted a sign in the billiard room of his home requiring guests to donate $1 to the cause. When his daughter Jean arrived at Stormfield in April 1909, she helped by collecting books for the library. After her death in December 1909, Mark Twain used money from the sale of Jean's farm for the library, and at that point dedicated the library to her memory, as the Jean Clemens Memorial Library.

The year after Twain's death in 1910, with additional funds from town residents, the original library was built. Later, when money was needed for library expenses, an old friend of Twain's, Andrew Carnegie was approached and he agreed to provide funds "in memory of his friendship with Mark Twain." For many years thereafter Mr. Carnegie provided funds to the Library. In 1972, a new wing was added. In 2000 there was a complete library renovation. The library now houses over 50,000 books, videos, records, books from Twain's personal library, and a collection of books by and about Twain. Services and programs offered by the library include:

Summer reading programs
Adult book discussion groups
Story hours for children
Annual December art show
Special guest speakers and exhibits
DVD rentals
Annual book sale of more than 100,000 items

THEY ALL LIVED IN REDDING

DISTINGUISHED AND WELL-KNOWN REDDINGITES

Maj. Gen. Samuel Holden Parsons—1778 to 1782, Military leader, lawyer, jurist, Commander under Gen. Israel Putnam. He first proposed the idea of a Continental Congress in 1774. He was appointed first Chief Judge to Northwest Territory (Ohio) (lived on Black Rock Turnpike)

Katherine Dreier—1905 to 1918, Dreier was a patron of the modern art movement in the U.S. She formed the Societe Anonyme and organized the International Exhibition of Modern Art in Brooklyn, New York in 1926 with Marcel Duchamp and Man Ray. She was also a key player in founding the Museum of Modern Art in New York City (lived on Marchant Rd until 1918 and later moved across the Danbury line to Long Ridge Rd where she entertained artists such as Marcel Duchamp and Man Ray)

Martha Lucas Pate—1940's to 1960's. She was the president successively of both Sweetbriar College and Radcliffe College. She was active on the board of the United Negro College Fund (lived on Putnam Park Rd)

Orville H. Schell, Jr.—1971 to 1987, Lawyer, human rights activist, founded Americas Watch, Chairman of Helsinki Watch (lived on Giles Hill Rd)

Hume Cronyn—1940's to 1950's, Theater, TV, radio, and film actor. Emmy and Tony Award winner, Academy Award nominee (lived on Stepney Rd)

Jessica Tandy—1940's to 1950's, Tony-winning actress for her performance as Blanche DuBois in the original *Broadway* production of "A Streetcar Named Desire". She was the oldest actor to ever win an Academy Award, for "Driving Miss Daisy." Emmy Award winner (lived on Stepney Rd)

ESSENTIAL TOWN SERVICES

The Town of Redding is run by an elected Three-person Board of Selectmen with a Board of Finance.

The Redding Board of Education oversees the elementary and middle schools; the Region 9 Board of Education oversees the operation of Joel Barlow High School for Redding and Easton, who share in the cost of the school based on the number of students each has in the school.

Conservation Commission
Planning Commission
Zoning Commission
All-volunteer fire companies
Police Department
911 Emergency Answering Service
EMS Paramedic program
Commission on the Elderly
Landfill/Recycling Program
Snowplowing services

The town is served by Danbury Hospital and Norwalk Hospital, both with excellent reputations.

THEY ALL LIVED IN REDDING

RECOGNIZED AND NOTEWORTHY REDDINGITES

Alvin Toffler—1980's to 1990's, Author of global best-selling books, "Future Shock" and "The Third Wave."

Perry J. Kaufman—2002 to present, Beginning his career as a "rocket scientist" in the aerospace industry, he worked on the navigation and control systems of the Gemini space program. Today he's a leading financial futures expert, financial educator, and writer.

Virginia Kirkus—1940's to 1980, Founded the Kirkus Review in 1933, the twice-monthly book review service that was an innovation in the field of publishing and selling books (lived on Stepney Rd)

James Grashow—1975 to present, Sculptor of environmental installations, woodcut artist.

Jack Lawrence—1980's to present, Composer of many of America's popular songs including "Tenderly," "All or Nothing At All" and "Beyond the Sea."

Paul Winter—1980's, Award-winning saxophonist, band leader of the Paul Winter Consort, composer (lived on Marchant Rd)

Michael Sovern—1993 to present, Former President of Columbia University, Chairman of the American Academy in Rome.

Mary Anne Guitar—1956 to present, Author, pioneer in land conservation, former First Selectman of Redding.

SCHOOLS OF EXCELLENCE

Redding's student population is served by three schools: Redding Elementary School, John Read Middle School, and Joel Barlow High School which is also the high school for neighboring Easton.

Recognized as a School of Excellence by the U.S. Department of Education, the high school offers a broad curriculum that includes an Advanced Placement program. Students participate in a wide range of sports, art, and music programs as well as a wide range of clubs—including the math team, chess club, and outreach clubs.

Over 80% of Redding high school graduates go on to higher education.

"Reaching Every Student" serves as the motto of the elementary school which offers a solid foundation in basic skills, art, music, physical education, health education, and computer programs; special tutorial programs for reading, math, and ESL; and an extended day program for children of working parents. There is an active Parent Teacher Association and many opportunities for parental involvement in the classroom.

Special education begins at the preschool level and continues through high school. Hot lunches and bus transportation are provided at all three schools.

There are six high-quality preschools in Redding as well as those in nearby towns.

College courses within an easy commute include:
Fairfield University
Norwalk Community College
Sacred Heart University (Fairfield)
University of Bridgeport
University of Connecticut at Stamford
Western Connecticut State University (Danbury)
Yale University (New Haven)
Southern Connecticut State University (New Haven)

There are also several other community colleges including Housatonic Valley Community College.

THEY ALL LIVED IN REDDING

RECOGNIZED AND NOTEWORTHY REDDINGITES

Mary Travers—1960's to present, Folk singer (of Peter, Paul and Mary) During its legendary career, the trio won five Grammys, produced five Top 10 albums and 13 Top 40 hits, of which 6 reached the Top 10—as well as six gold and three platinum albums.

Dick Morris—1985 to 2006, Political consultant, adviser to President Bill Clinton, author of many best-selling non-fiction books, columnist, TV commentator (lived on Beeholm Rd)

Eileen McGann—1985 to 2006, Attorney, political consultant with Dick Morris on global campaigns, co-author (with Dick Morris) of many best-selling non-fiction books, co-founded Vote.com, designed to give Internet users a voice on important public issues and other topics (lived on Beeholm Rd)

Tasha Tudor—1922 to 1938 then 1943 to 1944, Award-winning illustrator of nearly *one hundred children's books* and thousands of Christmas cards (lived on Tudor Lane)

Clementine Paddleford—1940's to 1970's, Food columnist, editor (lived on Cross Hwy)

Harry Edmonds, Sr.—1920's to 1950's, A founder of International House in New York City (lived in Redding Center)

Flannery O'Connor—1950's, Writer who completed over two dozen short stories and two novels (lived on Seventy Acres Rd)

Daryl Hall—1980's, Rock musician (of Hall and Oates) With over 60 million albums sold, Daryl Hall and John Oates have garnered a total of eight #1 hit singles along with dozens of hits throughout the 70's, 80's, 90's, including 2002's "Do It For Love," (lived on Topstone Rd)

Alvin Tresselt—1940's to 1960's, Founded Institute of Children's Literature, author (lived on Dorethy Rd)

DEVIL'S DEN AT SAUGATUCK RESERVOIR

NATURE PRESERVED AND ENJOYED

Redding encourages every resident to be active in preserving its rural character through the preservation of open space and antique buildings. Redding's commitment to preserving land in its natural state makes it unique to Fairfield County. Over 5.000 of the town's 20,000 acres are protected, providing seasonal enjoyments to residents and important conservation benefits. This land includes the Saugatuck Reservoir, two state parks, and land owned by the town and private groups (the Nature Conservancy, Connecticut Audubon Society, the Redding Land Trust).

***Devil's Den Nature Preserve*—**Features great hiking and scenic views of the Saugatuck Reservoir from the "Great Ledge."

Hiking Trails—Over 60 miles of trails have been blazed by volunteers through the open space of Redding, including natural landmarks such as the Great Ledge, Falls Hole, and Lonetown Marsh, as well as most of the 200-plus acres once owned by Mark Twain. "The Book of Trails" provides maps, history, and regulations for hiking, cross-country skiing, and horseback riding (published by the Redding Land Trust). This useful book can be purchased at the Mark Twain Library and at the Town Hall.

Topstone Park *in West Redding*—200-acre wooded public town park, once the private domain of the photographer Edward Steichen includes:

A small clear lake for swimming and canoeing
Trails for bicycling
Horseback riding
Picnic/barbecue area

STATE PARKS

ANNUAL REVOLUTIONARY WAR ENCAMPMENT AT PUTNAM PARK

Putnam Park — 183 acres, the first state park in Connecticut features:

* Cross-country skiing in winter.
* Hiking, picnicking, and fishing in summer.
* A statue of General Israel Putnam by Anna Hyatt Huntington and an historic museum containing remnants of Gen. Putnam's 1778-79 winter encampment.
* An annual reenactment of an historic Revolutionary War battle. Putnam Park is often referred to as "Connecticut's Valley Forge." It is also the first park in the state to be named an Archaeological Preserve.

ANNUAL REVOLUTIONARY WAR BATTLE REENACTMENT

Huntington State Park—Bequeathed by Archer M. Huntington, features:

* A small lake for kayaking and canoeing.
* Hiking trails and picnicking areas.

Highstead Arboretum—Beautiful displays of seasonal flowers, plants and trees that can be visited by appointment.

LOCAL FARMS

WARRUPS FARM FOR SUMMER CORN AND AUTUMN PUMPKINS

In Redding and nearby towns, families have the chance to pick their own fruits and vegetables, visit farm animals, and enjoy seasonal treats such as hayrides, maple sugaring, and Easter-egg hunts.

New Pond Farm has an award-winning dairy store where one can buy milk, cheese,and yogurt—and wool. 18th century Warrups Farm has organic vegetables for sale in the summertime, pumpkins and its own maple syrup in the fall. Another Reddingite, Phil Bronson also processes and sells maple syrup.

With two rivers and many ponds and streams lacing through Redding's backyards and open spaces, you don't have to look too hard to find a waterfall.

A WATERFALL IN POVERTY HOLLOW

THEY ALL LIVED IN REDDING

RECOGNIZED AND NOTEWORTHY REDDINGITES

Jeanette L. Gilder—1903 to 1916, First of the "literary colony." Critic, correspondent, literary and drama editor for the New York Herald. Friend of Mark Twain and Ida Tarbell, who lived nearby in Easton (lived on Black Rock Turnpike)

John Ward Stimson—c. 1878 to 1915—Author, lecturer, artist who founded Artist and Artisan School of New York and was director of the Arts Schools of the Metropolitan Museum (lived in Redding Center)

Hilary Knight—Illustrator of the "Eloise in Paris" children's books that were very popular in the 1960's. He illustrated over fifty books, nine of which he also wrote. His work also included record album covers and posters for the Broadway musicals "Half a Sixpence" and "Gypsy."

Ruth Stout—1950's to 1970's, Organic gardening guru who wrote many gardening books. Developed the "Stout Method" of gardening that utilizes "permanent mulch," "no dig" gardening process.

REDDING AROUND THE YEAR

Here's a brief roundup of some of the activities open to residents throughout the year.

Spring
Easter Egg Hunts
Spring Festivals
Pick your own at area farms
Tractor pull at the Historical Society
Memorial Day parade

ANNUAL MEMORIAL DAY PARADE WITH FIFE AND DRUM MARCHING BAND AT REDDING CENTER

Summer
Summer camp
Swimming and fishing at Topstone Lake
Tennis and swimming lessons
Summer theaters in nearby towns
Fire Station Cook-Out
Traveling circuses and festivals
Mark Twain Library Book Sale
Georgetown Street Festival.
Free Concerts on the Green
Best ice cream at Dr. Mike's in Bethel and Monroe and Ferris Acres Creamery in Newtown

SIGN ANNOUNCING FREE WEEKLY SUMMER CONCERTS ON THE GREEN

Autumn
Hayrides
Haunted houses
Pumpkin picking at area farms
Fall Festivals
Halloween Parties
December Art Show at the library
Arts and Crafts Fair in Redding Center

**ANNUAL AUTUMN ARTS AND CRAFTS FAIR
AT REDDING CENTER**

Winter
Christmas tree lighting and caroling at Redding Center
Sledding and cross-country skiing at Putnam Park
Cut-your-own Christmas trees at local farms
Volleyball and aerobics
Story Hour at the library
School concerts, plays, and sports
Swimming at Meadow Ridge retirement home

THEY ALL LIVED IN REDDING

RECOGNIZED AND NOTEWORTHY REDDINGITES

Father John Guiliani—1980's to present, Benedictine priest, Native-American-style artist and art collector, commissioned to paint the banner in Siena, Italy's Palio.

Robert Natkin—1980's to present, Abstract painter whose work is associated with Abstract expressionism, Color field painting, and Lyrical Abstraction. Since the early 1950's he has created paintings which are represented in the permanent collections of major museums as well as in corporate and private collections. His work has also been exhibited in leading galleries in the U.S., Europe and Japan.

Judith Dolnick—1970's to present, Noted watercolor and acrylic artist who paints on paper and canvas. Her works are in the collections of the Metropolitan Museum and Museum of Modern Art in New York, Hirshhorn Museum in DC, and the Art Institute of Chicago. She has also exhibited in many galleries throughout the world and her work is represented in many private collections.

Clayton Knight—1940's to 1969. Artist, aviation illustrator, awarded The Order of the British Empire (O.B.E.) for conspicuous service to England's cause in both World Wars (lived on Umpawaug Rd)

Kathy Anderson,—1979 to present, Artist, won the Portrait Award at National Arts Club in NYC, one of thirty national artists invited to participate in the Telluride Plein Air Festival in Colorado.

Julian Barry—2001 to present, Playwright, screenplay writer, stage manager, actor. Wrote the Broadway drama, "Lenny" and the screenplays for "Lenny" (for which he won an Oscar), "The River," "Rhinoceros," and "Me, Myself and I."

Barry Levinson—1990's to present, Two-time Oscar-winning motion picture director, producer, writer for such films as "Rain Man," 'Good Morning Vietnam," "Diner" and "Avalon."

THEY ALL LIVED IN REDDING

RECOGNIZED AND NOTEWORTHY REDDINGITES

Stuart Linder—2002 to 2005, Oscar-winning film editor for the motion picture "Grand Prix" in 1966. Edited many films for Director Barry Levinson (lived on Poverty Hollow Rd)

Meat Loaf—(aka. Marvin Lee Aday)—1980's to 1990's - Rock musician and composer, his operatic rock album entitled, "Bat Out Of Hell", has sold 35 million copies worldwide. He coached the Redding school softball team, (lived on Orchard Drive)

Paul Caponigro—late 1960's to 1970's, Award-winning silver gelatin landscape photographer (lived near Little River)

Fred Otnes—1980's to present, Collage artist, winner of more than 150 corporate design awards.

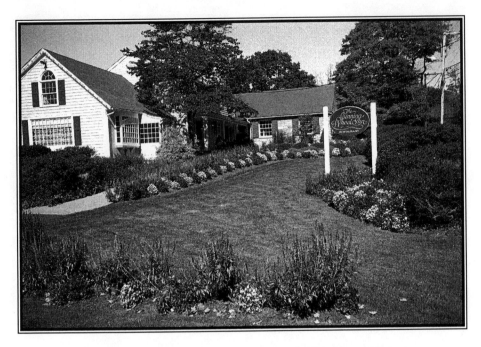

HISTORIC COUNTRY INN IN REDDING RIDGE

Redding's Neighbors
In West Redding, Redding Ridge, and Georgetown there are:
Pharmacies
Banks
Convenience stores
Restaurants (including an historic country inn)
Gift shops

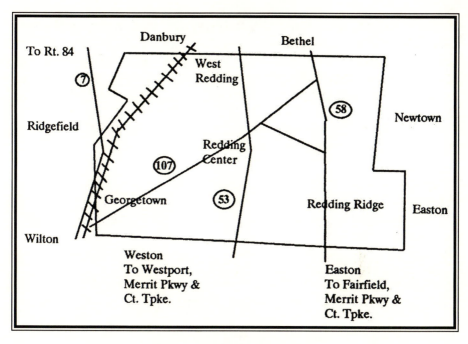

MAP OF REDDING AREA

Additional food shopping, theaters, parks, restaurants and professional services can be found close by in neighboring Ridgefield, Bethel, Wilton, Danbury, Easton, Monroe, and Newtown.

* 10-20 minutes to Branchville, Bethel, Danbury, Wilton, Easton, Monroe, Newtown, and Ridgefield
Weir Farm Museum: Former home and studio of American Impressionist Artist, Julian Alden Weir (Branchville), the only National Historic site in Connecticut
Bethel and Danbury movie theaters
Danbury Mall has many major chain stores
Danbury Airport for private aircraft
Danbury Hospital
Wilton Mall
Restaurants of all types
Wilton, Easton, and Bethel Libraries
YMCA (Danbury)
Aldrich Contemporary Art Museum (Ridgefield)
Ridgefield Playhouse and Ridgefield Theater Barn for theater, concerts, and movies
Silverman's Petting Zoo, apple cider mill and farm stand (Easton)

* 20-35 minutes to Norwalk, Bridgeport, Westport, Brookfield and New York State
Norwalk Hospital
SoNo Maritime Center (South Norwalk)
SoNo Oyster Festival (South Norwalk)
SoNo Arts Festival (South Norwalk)
Discovery Museum (Bridgeport)
Barnum Museum (Bridgeport)
Bridgeport Zoo
Bridgeport Theater
Westport Country Playhouse
Sherwood Island State Park (Westport—oldest Connecticut state park)
Candlewood Playhouse (New Fairfield)
Quassy Amusement Park (Middlebury)
Caramoor Music Festival (Katonah, NY)
Katonah Museum
Candlewood Lake for motorboating, sailing, fishing

* 45 minutes to New Haven and Bristol
Lake Compounce Family Theme Park (Bristol)
Long Wharf Theater (New Haven)
Peabody Museum of Natural History (New Haven)
Yale University (New Haven)
Yale Art Museum (New Haven)
Museum of British Art (New Haven)
Yale Summer Arts Festival (New Haven)

* 1-1/2 hours to New York City
Trains daily from West Redding, Branchville, Bridgeport, Fairfield, Bethel, Westport, to New York City

THEY ALL LIVED IN REDDING

RECOGNIZED AND NOTEWORTHY REDDINGITES

Howard Fast—1980's—Historical novelist and TV writer whose most famous books are "Spartacus" (made into a major motion picture) and "April Morning." (lived on Cross Hwy)

Jane Hamilton Merritt—1980'S to present. Journalist, twice nominated for a Nobel Peace Prize for her humanitarian work for the Hmong people of northern Laos, Pulitzer Prize nominee.

George Leland Hunter—1910's to 1927, American authority on decorative art. His writings appeared in many magazines and several books. He wrote "Tapestries, their Origin, History, and Renaissance" (1912), regarded as finest book in English on the subject (lived on Mark Twain Lane)

Michael Strange (aka Blanche Oelrichs)—1940's, Playwright, poet, actress, once married to actor John Barrymore (lived on Rock House Rd)

Mark Pinter—1987 to present, TV, film, and stage actor, and director. Starred in many daytime TV series such as "Another World" and "All My Children."

Colleen Zenk Pinter—1987 to present—TV, theater actress. She has had a leading role since 1978 in the daytime TV series, "As the World Turns."

Carmen Mathews—1950's to 1995, Stage, TV and film actress. Appeared in hundreds of TV, Hollywood, and Broadway productions, founded Redding's New Pond Farm and Education Center (lived on Marchant Rd)

Susan B. Durkee—1975 to present, Award-winning artist whose paintings have been featured on television shows, in many publications including National Geographic, has had many corporate commissions.

THEY ALL LIVED IN REDDING

RECOGNIZED AND NOTEWORTHY REDDINGITES

Marc Mellon—1989 to present, Representational sculptor. His commissions have included busts of Pope John Paul II, President George H.W. Bush and President Lee of Taiwan.

Babette Bloch—1989 to present, Award-winning sculptor who is a pioneer in laser-cut stainless steel sculpture. Her works include site-specific one-of-a-kind commissions for public spaces, and limited editions.

David Heald—1994 to present, Chief Photographer for Guggenheim Museum of Art in New York City, created photography book, "Architecture of Silence."

Edward Dzubak—1995 to present, Three-time Daytime Drama Emmy Award-winning TV composer, has composed music for films and many global broadcasts.

Julie Kavner—1980's to 1990's, Emmy Award-winning actress for TV's "Rhoda" series, appeared in 5 Woody Allen films, created the voice of Marge Simpson on "The Simpsons" TV series.

HISTORICAL PLAQUE ON REDDING GREEN

HISTORY OF REDDING

1687—In the seventeenth century, Major Nathan Gold, colonial Deputy Governor, established first farm in Redding along the Saugatuck River

1714—John Read Esq. established 500-acre Lonetown Manor by deed with local Sagamore Indian Chickens Warrups

1729—Redding became a parish of Fairfield

1767—Incorporated as Town of Redding, separating itself from Fairfield

April 25, 1777—General Tryon and British troops marched through Redding Ridge toward Danbury. 16 local militia members were captured following a skirmish and later imprisoned

ANNUAL EDUCATION PROGRAM DESCRIBING GENERAL PUTNAM AND HIS TROOPS' 1778-79 ENCAMPMENT IN PUTNAM PARK

1778-1779—General Israel Putnam and his troops, the Left Wing of the Continental Army, suffered a harsh winter encamped in Redding, now commemorated as Putnam Park

1779—Two of Gen. Putnam's soldiers were executed by Putnam for spying and desertion at what is now called Gallows Hill Road, to set an example to other troops

Reverend Beach of the Episcopal Church was threatened for praying for King George III of England; a bullet fired at him during a service is still embedded in a tablet in Christ Church

1789—Jesse Lee, an itinerant Methodist preacher, converted Aaron Sanford to Methodism, making him one of the earliest converts in New England (NOTE: John Wesley brought Methodism from England to the Carolinas in the 1740s). The first camp meetings took place in Brookside Park; stone pillars in West Redding Center are what remain of the entrance to the park

1827—Benjamin Gilbert and his son-in-law Sturges Bennett contrived a loom to weave the first sieves out of horse hair, later of wire. Many Scandinavian immigrants settled here to work in the large brick factory in Georgetown that operated until the 1980's

1800's—Small-scale manufacture of buttons (Stepney Road), pins and brass items, shirts, bricks, carriages and hats (Hattertown Road). There was also lime production (Limekiln Road), quarrying and iron smelting (Old Foundry Road)

1877—Reverend Dickinson discovered new minerals, including one which was named Reddingite

Early **1900's**—Redding became a country retreat for New Yorkers and others as farming and industry declined

1940—Bridgeport Hydraulic Company completed purchases of some 2,800 acres, then known as Redding Glen, and turned it into the Saugatuck Reservoir

1965—The Redding Land Trust was formed to purchase land to be preserved as open space and the town adopts an open space plan. By 2008, almost 30% of the town's acreage was town-owned or otherwise preserved

THEY ALL LIVED IN REDDING

RECOGNIZED AND NOTEWORTHY REDDINGITES

Harold Foster—1944 to 1982, Creator and cartoonist of Prince Valiant comic strip from 1937 to 1971.

Hope Lange—TV, theater, and motion picture actress, 1957 Oscar-nominee for "Peyton Place," won an Emmy for TV series, "Ghost and Mrs. Muir," 1970's TV series with Dick Van Dyke (was born in Redding Ridge).

Victoria Wyndham—2003 to present, Theater and TV Actress, director, producer, painter, sculptor. For more than twenty-five years she starred in daytime TV series, "Another World."

Per Ola and Emily D'Aulaire,—1971 to present, Writers on travel, nature, and popular culture, book authors. They received wide recognition for their 2002 Smithsonian Magazine article on the first hand-written bible.

John Walsh—(1973 to 1993), In 1978 his award-winning Black Swan Press was founded as the first Redding-based publishing imprint and was continued until 1997 by co-founder PATRICIA WALSH SOVERN (1973 to present). They published works by Ezra Pound, D.H. Lawrence, Lawrence Durell, and Auguste Rodin.

Frank Doelger—1980's to 2005, Emmy Award-winning producer for HBO Winston Churchill series, HBO "John Adams," "Rome" series, (lived on Poverty Hollow Rd)

Frank Hawks—1930's, Aviator and multiple air speed record holder. Friend of Will Rogers, took Amelia Earhart on her first flight (lived on Redding Rd)

Rear Admiral Lauren Strong McCready—1980's to 2007, Instrumental in establishing Engineering Department at the King's Point Merchant Marine Academy in 1942 (lived on Gallows Hill Rd)

THEY ALL LIVED IN REDDING

RECOGNIZED AND NOTEWORTHY REDDINGITES

C.D. Mallory—1920's to 1940's, Mystic Seaport founder, founded and owned Mallory Steamship Lines (lived on Marchant Rd)

Elsie M. Hill—1920's to 1930's, Women's Suffragette. *An organizer for the National Women's Party. She was jailed in February 1919 in Boston for her participation in the "welcome" demonstration of President Woodrow Wilson* (lived on Seventy Acres Rd)

Julie Hagerty,—1980's, film and TV actress, starred in such films as "Airplane" and "Lost in America" (lived on Marchant Rd)

Holly Keller—1980's to 1990's, Award-winning author of more than 25 children's books, illustrator, creator of popular "Farfallina & Marcel" books.

Joan Walsh Anglund—1950's to 1990's, children's book author and illustrator of more than 90 books including "A Friend Is Someone Who Likes You" and "Brave Cowboy." (lived on Black Rock Turnpike)

Arthur Shilstone—1980's to present, Watercolor artist whose paintings are in many museum and private collections.

Louis G. Cowan—1970's, TV producer. Created "$64,000 Question" and produced "The Quiz Kids" (lived on Lonetown Rd)

Diana Canova—1980's to present, TV and theater actress who starred in TV sitcoms including "Soap" and "Throb."

Elliott Scheiner—1980's to present, Five-time Grammy-winning music producer for such performers as Ricky Martin, Sting, Fleetwood Mac.

THEY ALL LIVED IN REDDING

RECOGNIZED AND NOTEWORTHY REDDINGITES

Andy Powell—1980's to present, Lead guitarist and vocalist for the rock band, Wishbone Ash. Named to the all-time top-five guitarists by Rolling Stone magazine.

Lawrence Kudlow—1980's to present, Economist, TV commentator, Associate Director for Economics and Planning for President Ronald Reagan.

Jane and Michael Stern—1980's to present, Authors of more than *20 books about America*. Their "Roadfood" column for Gourmet magazine has won three James Beard Awards. Their "Roadfood" segments have appeared on the Television Food Network.

Enoch Light—1970's, Orchestra leader of The Light Brigade and their hit "Persuasive Percussion" music albums.

Ruth Chatterton—1950's, Writer, film, TV and theater actress in such Broadway hits as "Tomorrow and Tomorrow" in 1932 and the title role in "Lily Turner" in 1933 (lived on Sanfordtown Rd)

Richie Blackmore—1980's, lead guitarist with rock group, Deep Purple (lived on Tunxis Trail)

Roma Gans—1970's to 1980's, Teachers College pioneer in reading education, children's book writer, *co-founder of the Let's-Read-and-Find-Out Science series.*

Anatole Broyard—1980's, NY Times literary critic, author (lived on Lonetown Rd)

To protect the privacy of those Reddingites who presently live in Redding their home addresses are omitted in this publication.

ANECDOTES

* In 1985 I attended a party at the Mark Twain Library to honor Mark Twain's birthday. At the party, Mr. Hawthorne Deming, a great-grandson of the noted American writer, Nathaniel Hawthorne, related a story about an event that took place when he was about five years old. Mr. Deming lived in Redding since he was born here in 1904. He specifically recollected a time when he was sitting on the lap of a man who was dressed all in white and had lots of hair on his face. He distinctly remembered that the man had an unpleasant smell about him (like cigars?). When he was older Mr. Deming's parents confirmed that he actually sat on Mark Twain's lap at a Redding picnic. At this one moment, two generations of American literary history were brought together in Redding.

* Reddingites trade stories of how the Poverty Hollow section of Redding Ridge got its name. One such story took place in the 19th century where there was a button factory in Redding Ridge. Legend has it that one Sunday after services, the minister of the local church shook his donations box and happily exclaimed that it sounded full. When he opened it he found it full of buttons, whereupon he declared, "This surely is poverty hollow"—and the name stuck forever after.

* As the story goes, the composer Charles Ives was outraged when airplanes began flying over Redding, and whenever he heard one he would come out and shake his fist at it and shout "Get off my property!" He didn't want anything to disrupt the peaceful country ambiance of Umpawaug Hill which he loved.

* You might not be aware that long-time Reddingite Edward Steichen's sister was married to renowned poet Carl Sandburg. The Sandburgs sometimes visited Steichen in West Redding. In fact, according to what Steichen's widow, Joanna Steichen recently told me, it was Sandburg who introduced her to his brother-in-law, Edward Steichen in 1959. After their marriage, the Steichens continued to live in West Redding. When Steichen died at his home of heart failure on March 25, 1973 at the age of 94, at his request, he was cremated. He had already selected the exact spot on his property where he wanted his ashes to be buried. In Joanna Steichen's book, "Steichen's Legacy," she wrote, "Halfway up a wooded hill on the

way to the house stood a huge mound of boulders unlikely ever to be moved no matter who owned the property. All the ashes were to be buried at the base of the outcropping. Then a small brass plaque giving his name and the dates, was to be attached to one of the biggest boulders. And so it was done exactly as Steichen had requested."

Joanna Steichen generously granted me permission to use her exact words in this volume.

In 1995, Loren Zeller and his wife purchased part of the former Steichen property, the second owners since the Steichens. As Mr. Zeller recently related to me from where he now lives in Arizona, when he purchased the house the entire garden area was covered with underbrush. Two years later, in 1997, Zeller started a major project to clear all the brush and that uncovered the large boulder and plaque. Until I told Zeller in July 2006 that Mrs. Steichen confirmed that that was the actual burial place, Zeller had only surmised it might be. Today, Steichen's final resting place remains on private property and has been tastefully and beautifully landscaped by the present owners.

* What do you think Leonard Bernstein and Jascha Heifetz did on Sunday afternoons in Redding during the early 1950's? They went for a 'jam session' in Gladys's barn on Huckleberry Road. That is Gladys Swarthout, former Metropolitan Opera mezzo soprano, who owned our house on Huckleberry Road. It was listed under the name of Chapman, her husband. On one of those Sundays, this music group was joined by another renowned violinist, Yehudi Menuhin, a good friend of Heifetz, who happened to be in town for the day.

—*This anecdote was contributed by Mr. Han van Oostendorp of Huckleberry Road*

ACKNOWLEDGEMENTS

***Susan Wolf**—whose encouragement and advice made this book a reality
***Sarah Tison and Joan Demaree**—for advising me of the need for this book
***Charley Couch**—whose consistent encouragement, advice, direction, and vetting of names. places, and history have been invaluable
***John DeCesare**—whose creative contributions, generosity, and encouragement have been invaluable over the years and especially for this book
***Bob Morton**—whose guidance, suggestions and advice have made this book what I hoped it would be
***Carol Morgan**—whose guidance, editing, suggestions, and encouragement have been invaluable
***Sonya Hamlin**—whose suggestions and support have been invaluable
***Joan Ensor**—for her vetting of names and places to ensure accuracy
***Heather Morgan**—whose support and suggestions have been invaluable
***Joanna Steichen**—for her background information, advice, and permission to include the excerpts from her book
***Mary Anne Guitar**—for her vetting of names and places to ensure accuracy
***Pam and Greg Berry**—for the generosity of their advice and time
***June Myles**—for her support and assistance in finding the Steichen lore
***Brent Colley**—for his support and keeping the accuracy of this book on track
***Loren Zeller**—for his invaluable advice about the Steichen property
***Hugh Karraker**—for his support and vetting of names and places
***Susan Durkee**—for her support and vetting of names and places and especially **Google**

And the many people from all over the US who contributed names, addresses and details of notable Reddingites.

I welcome comments, corrections, and additions of other notable Reddingites and anecdotes from my readers by emailing me at: *dennispaget@gmail.com*

Links to more Redding information on the Internet:
http://www.historyofredding.com
(Created and supervised by Brent Colley)

http://www.townofreddingct.org
http://www.acorn-online.com/ (The Redding Pilot)